LAUGH
-OUT-
LOUD

JOKES FOR KIDS

WOULD
YOU
RATHER

LAUGH
-OUT-
LOUD
JOKES FOR KIDS

WOULD YOU RATHER

ROB ELLIOTT

HARPER

An Imprint of HarperCollinsPublishers

Library of Congress Control Number: 2023936923
ISBN 978-0-06-328773-0 (paper-over-board)
ISBN 978-0-06-328776-1 (pbk.)

Typography by Catherine Lee
23 24 25 26 27 LBC 5 4 3 2 1

First Edition

LAUGH -OUT- LOUD

JOKES FOR KIDS

WOULD YOU RATHER

Would you rather

ride on the back of a T. rex

or

fly on the back of a pterodactyl?

Q: What do you call twin dinosaurs?

A: A pair-odactyls!

Q: Why can't you hear a pterodactyl go to the bathroom?

A: The *p* is silent!

Would you rather

own a pet otter

or

own a pet zebra?

Would you rather

live in the world of Star Wars

or

live in the world of Lord of the Rings?

Would you rather

climb a mountain

or

sail across the ocean?

Q: Why is tennis such a noisy sport?

A: The players raise a racket!

Q: Why are boxers great comedians?

A: They know how to deliver a punch

line!

Would you rather

go to math class in your swimsuit

or

go to gym class in a tuxedo?

Would you rather

pilot a plane in the sky

or

steer a submarine underwater?

Would you rather

soar like an eagle

or

swim like a dolphin?

Would you rather

eat pizza for dinner each night for the

rest of your life

or

eat tacos for dinner each night for the

rest of your life?

Q: Why is spaghetti the smartest food?

A: It's always using its noodle!

Q: Where do you learn to make a banana split?

A: In sundae school!

Q: When does your dinner never stay hot?

A: When it's chili.

Would you rather

predict the future

or

change the past?

Would you rather

read people's thoughts

or

be invisible?

Would you rather

be a popular singer

or

be a famous actor?

Would you rather

have webbed feet like a duck

or

have webbed hands like a frog?

Would you rather

eat fifty cookies in one sitting

or

eat fifty candy bars at once?

Would you rather

not celebrate Christmas for one year

or

skip your birthday for one year?

Would you rather

get fifty presents for Christmas

or

go on an amazing trip for the holiday?

Would you rather

eat fruitcake every day in December

or

drink eggnog each day for the month?

Would you rather

meet Frosty the Snowman

or

meet Rudolph the Red-nosed

Reindeer?

Would you rather

live in a big city

or

live on a ranch?

Would you rather

sing every time you opened your

mouth

or

dance every time you moved your

feet?

Would you rather

eat fried worms

or

eat fried cockroaches?

Would you rather

fly as fast as Superman

or

run as fast as the Flash?

Would you rather

live at a zoo

or

live at an aquarium?

Would you rather

wear a clown nose every day

or

wear a fake mustache all the time?

Would you rather

eat four raw eggs

or

lay four eggs?

Would you rather

wear a suit and work at a desk

or

wear a uniform and work outside?

Would you rather

be a firefighter

or

be an astronaut?

Would you rather

breathe underwater

or

walk on water?

Would you rather

float like a balloon

or

bounce like a ball?

Would you rather

spray water from your fingers

or

shoot fire from your toes?

Would you rather

eat a booger sandwich

or

eat an earwax sandwich?

Would you rather

find a pot of gold

or

discover a genie's lamp?

- -

Q: Why can't trees be trusted?

A: They are shady!

Q: Why did the bride and groom

go to a cheese factory after the

wedding?

A: They wanted to grow mold together!

Q: What did the drum say to the

guitar before the concert?

A: "Don't fret!"

Would you rather

live in a tree house in the jungle

or

live in an igloo in the Arctic?

Would you rather

eat breakfast for dinner every night

or

eat dinner for breakfast every

morning?

Would you rather

get paid a little to do the job of your

dreams

or

make a lot of money at a job you hate?

Would you rather

eat a meal on a dirty plate

or

eat off the floor?

Would you rather

talk like Donald Duck

or

have a voice like Goofy?

Would you rather

have quills like a porcupine

or

have a tail that sprays like a skunk?

Would you rather

wear fancy clothes all day

or

dress in pajamas all day?

Q: How does a hamburger introduce

his girlfriend?

A: "Meet Patty."

Q: What kind of doctor is Dr Pepper?

A: He's a fizz-ician!

Q: What do bunnies say before they eat?

A: "Lettuce pray!"

Knock, knock.

Who's there?

Figs.

Figs who?

Figs the doorbell already!

Would you rather

hiccup for ten minutes of every hour

or

sneeze for ten minutes of every hour?

Would you rather

have a spider in your bathroom

or

have a mouse in your kitchen?

Would you rather

wear a scuba diver's wet suit to class

or

wear an astronaut's space suit to

school?

Would you rather

put hot sauce on all your food

or

put honey on everything you eat?

Would you rather

go skiing in the winter

or

go waterskiing in the summer?

Would you rather

live in a mansion in the country

or

live in a penthouse in a big city?

Would you rather

live in a house made of cheese

or

live in a house made of Jell-O?

Would you rather

stay inside and never get to go out

or

stay outside and never get to come in?

Would you rather

drive a race car

or

operate a bulldozer?

Q: What kind of dog does Frosty have for a pet?

A: A Saint Brrr-nard!

Q: What does a knitter and a gym's personal trainer have in common?

A: They both make heavy sweaters!

Q: What did the lion say after he ate the dentist?

A: "He was so filling!"

Q: What do you get when you cross a chicken and a baseball player?

A: A fowl ball!

Q: Why do snowplow drivers make so many friends?

A: They know how to break the ice.

Q: What is a boxer's favorite candy?

A: Jawbreakers!

Q: What did the mommy noodle say to the baby noodle?

A: "It's pasta your bedtime!"

Q: Why do skeletons make great comedians?

A: They're humerus!

Q: What do you give your cat when it's sick?

A: A purr-scription!

Q: Why can't snowmen ever make up their mind?

A: They're flaky!

Q: Why did the pony get a time-out?

A: It was horsing around!

Would you rather

have X-ray vision

or

supersonic hearing?

Q: What did the surgeon say to the patient who didn't want stitches?

A: "Suture self!"

Would you rather

speak five different languages

or

play five different instruments?

Q: **What does a bee put on its cupcakes?**

A: Fro-sting!

Q: **What did the mommy wasp say to the baby wasp?**

A: "Bee-have!"

Q: Why was the eye doctor so shy at parties?

A: He didn't want to make a spectacle of himself.

Q: Why was the duck so happy after its checkup?

A: It got a clean bill of health!

Q: Why couldn't the bee get along with its neighbors?

A: They wouldn't mind their own buzz-ness!

Q: How do you make a meteorologist mad?

A: You steal their thunder!

Q: Why did the meteorologist call in sick to work?

A: He was feeling under the weather!

Q: What did the zombie call the martial arts instructor?

A: "Kung food!"

Q: What do zombies look for at a farmers market?

A: Farmers!

Q: Why did the nurse become an artist?

A: She knew how to draw blood!

Knock, knock.

Who's there?

Wheeze.

Wheeze who?

Wheeze going to tell some more jokes!

Q: Why was the panda asked to join the choir?

A: They needed more bear-itones.

Q: How does a grizzly build its house?

A: With its bear hands!

Q: What's the most boring thing to read in the library?

A: The snooze-paper!

Q: What kind of dinosaur sleeps all the time?

A: A bronto-snore-us.

Q: Why did the man buy new pants every payday?

A: His money always burned a hole in his pocket!

Q: Why did the girl always get straight A's in school?

A: She used a ruler.

Would you rather

use a pacifier all day

or

be pushed in a stroller all day?

Q: What will happen if you take a skunk along on your trip?

A: Your vacation will stink!

Q: What is an ogre's favorite kind of tea?

A: Nas-tea!

Q: What do boxers eat for dinner?

A: Black-eyed peas and fruit punch!

Would you rather

meet the tooth fairy

or

meet the Easter bunny?

Would you rather

have a strawberry milkshake

or

drink a strawberry smoothie?

Would you rather

wear flip-flops in the snow

or

wear snow boots at the beach?

Would you rather

have mashed potatoes with chocolate

   syrup

or

put gravy on your ice cream?

Would you rather

wake up at the same time each

morning

or

go to bed at the same time every

night?

Would you rather

cook the food for a restaurant

or

serve the food at a restaurant?

Would you rather

swim all day at a water park

or

jump all day at a trampoline park?

Would you rather

never use a cell phone

or

never watch TV?

Q: Why didn't the oyster like public speaking?

A: It would always clam up!

Q: What do you get when you combine a tuna and a clown?

A: A jolly-fish!

Would you rather

skip taking showers for a month

or

never brush your teeth for a month?

Q: Why did the pony need a drink of water?

A: It was feeling a little horse!

Would you rather

eat a stick of butter

or

eat a cup of mayonnaise?

Would you rather

mow five lawns in one day

or

vacuum five houses in a day?

Q: Why did the surfer bring his surfboard to the hair salon?

A: He was looking for a permanent wave!

Q: What do you call the president's boat?

A: Leader-ship!

Q: Why did the snowman eat ten snow cones?

A: He wanted a brain freeze!

Q: Why did the baker go to the square dance?

A: So she could dough-si-dough!

Would you rather

wrap one hundred Christmas presents

or

decorate twenty-five Christmas trees?

Q: Why did Father forget to buy

more peanut butter?

A: He was spread too thin!

Would you rather

shout every time you have something

to say

or

whisper whenever you speak?

Q: Why was the library so tall?

A: They kept adding stories to it!

Would you rather

eat an entire pie

or

eat a whole cake?

Would you rather

eat a jar of mustard

or

drink a bottle of ketchup?

Would you rather

have pancakes with no syrup

or

cereal with no milk?

Q: Why did the librarian keep all the books to herself?

A: Because she was shelf-ish!

Would you rather

have your own pet dinosaur

or

have a dragon for a pet?

Q: Why didn't the moon eat dessert?

A: Because it was full.

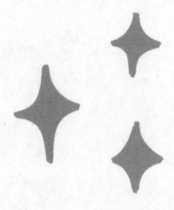

Would you rather

keep yawning all day

or

have the hiccups all day?

Would you rather

have darkness all day long

or

have the sun shining all night?

Would you rather

be six inches tall

or

grow to nine feet tall?

Would you rather

have a nose like an elephant

or

have a neck like a giraffe?

Would you rather

spend the day at the library

or

visit a museum for the day?

Would you rather

go hike the trails all day

or

ride your bike all day?

Q: What kind of monkey can fly?

A: A hot-air baboon!

Q: Why do bananas make bad friends?

A: They always split!

Q: Why did the firefighter quit his job?

A: He felt burned out!

Q: Why did the hamburger take the stand?

A: The lawyer wanted to grill it!

Q: What do you get when you cross a scientist and a stick of gum?

A: An experi-mint!

Q: Why was the doctor mad at the teacher?

A: She kept testing his patients!

Q: What do you call a cow who does yoga?

A: Flexi-bull!

Q: What part of a skunk smells the best?

A: Its nose!

Q: Which is the meanest kind of amphibian?

A: A bully-frog!

Would you rather

go without running water

or

get by without electricity?

Q: Why do trees make great dentists?

A: They get to the root of the problem!

Would you rather

drink a jar of pickle juice

or

drink a bottle of salad dressing?

Would you rather

eat a jar of peanut butter

or

eat a jar of strawberry jam?

Q: Why did the clock go on vacation?

A: It was all wound up!

Q: What kind of snake comes out after it rains?

A: The rain-boa!

Q: Why were the elephants embarrassed at the pool?

A: They kept dropping their trunks!

Q: Why was the art teacher so popular?

A: She knew how to draw a crowd!

Would you rather

have two thousand dollars now to
spend however you like

or

have ten thousand dollars waiting for
you in ten years?

Q: Why do cats make great bakers?

A: They like to work from scratch!

Would you rather

give up treats and sweets

or

stop eating chips and fries?

Would you rather

have bad breath

or

have stinky feet?

Would you rather

eat a bag of marshmallows

or

eat a package of chocolate bars?

Q: What is a monkey's favorite vegetable?

A: Zoo-chini!

Q: How did the turtle call its mom?

A: It used its shell phone!

Knock, knock.

Who's there?

Dude.

Dude who?

Don't be gross!

Q: What do a chef and a plumber have in common?

A: They both know how to fix leeks!

Q: What kind of travelers never get upset?

A: No-mads!

Q: Why did the orange juice get straight A's in school?

A: It knew how to concentrate!

Would you rather

play three rounds of paintball

or

play three rounds of laser tag?

Q: Why did the cheese go to the gym every day?

A: It wanted to get shredded!

Q: What did the puppy have to do before he went on a walk?

A: It asked his paw if it was okay!

Q: How do golfers have fun with their daughters?

A: They have tee parties!

Q: What goes tick, tick, ruff, ruff?

A: A watchdog!

Knock, knock.

Who's there?

Toad.

Toad who?

Toad you I'd come knocking today!

Q: What do snowmen like to eat at a barbecue?

A: Cold slaw.

Would you rather

lose your teeth

or

lose your hair?

Q: What did the shoe say to the foot?

A: "Put a sock in it!"

Q: What kind of nuts have bad allergies?

A: Cashews!

Q: What happened to the sick noodle?

A: It pasta way!

Would you rather

have your own roller coaster

or

have a waterslide of your own?

Knock, knock.

Who's there?

Window.

Window who?

Window I get to tell another joke?

Q: Why don't amoebas have any friends?

A: They're cell-fish!

Q: What is a caveman's favorite lunch?

A: A club sandwich!

Would you rather

be someone's personal chef

or

be someone's chauffeur?

Would you rather

get eggs from your own chickens

or

milk your own cow?

Q: Why did the polar bear cancel its date?

A: It got cold feet!

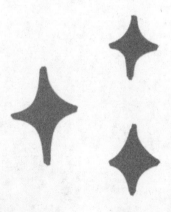

- -

Would you rather

live in a world where nobody is honest

or

live in a world where everybody says

what they really think?

Q: What did the glue say to the paper?

A: "Let's stick together!"

Q: Where did the sailboat go when it got sick?

A: To the dock!

Q: What happened when the tiger went shopping at the department store?

A: People got mall-ed!

Q: Why do ducks make great comedians?

A: Because they'll quack you up!

Would you rather

have your own butler

or

have a personal limo driver?

Would you rather

live in a world with no books

or

live in a world with no movies?

Would you rather

have a bad hair day

or

have bad breath?

Q: How did the stadium catch on fire?

A: With a soccer match!

Q: Why did Einstein carry an umbrella?

A: He was brainstorming!

Q: Why are toads so good at baseball?

A: They always catch the fly balls!

Kid 1: I'm not a robot!

Kid 2: R2!

Would you rather

make it snow whenever you want

or

make the sun come out any time you
  like?

Q: What do you get when you combine bread, cheese, and a kazoo?

A: A hum sandwich!

Q: What do you get when you combine a beetle with a cat?

A: A litterbug.

Would you rather

be able to fast-forward your life

or

make time go by more slowly?

Q: Why is Jack Frost a good

salesman?

A: He's not afraid of making cold calls!

Would you rather

feed all the animals at the zoo

or

test-drive all the cars at the racetrack?

Would you rather

stay dry in the rain

or

stay warm in the snow?

Q: What did the basketball player name his son?

A: Duncan!

Q: Why wouldn't anyone play soccer with the pig?

A: It kept hogging the ball.

Knock, knock.

Who's there?

Irish.

Irish who?

Irish you'd tell me more jokes!

Q: What does a garbage collector eat on his lunch break?

A: Junk food!

Q: What did one hat say to the other hat?

A: "You stay here, and I'll go on ahead!"

Q: Why couldn't the fish decide what to eat for dinner?

A: It kept floundering!

Q: What do sailors like to watch on TV?

A: Dock-umentaries!

Q: How did the pig feel when its dinner was late?

A: Disgruntled!

Q: When is a pig a tattletale?

A: When it squeals on you!

Q: Why did the pig go to the store for eggs, sugar, and flour?

A: Because it was bacon!

Q: What do you call a penguin in the Bahamas?

A: Lost!

Q: What happened to the ghosts at their performance?

A: They got booed off the stage!

Q: What kind of bugs like sushi?

A: Wasa-bees!

Q: What do artists do to relax?

A: They draw a bath!

Q: What do grizzlies eat for

breakfast?

A: Bear-ries!

Q: Why did the businessman buy an apple orchard?

A: He thought it would be a fruitful venture!

Q: Why was the computer cold?

A: It left too many windows open!

Q: What do you call a yeti that works out at the gym?

A: An abdominal snowman!

Q: Why can't vampires pay attention at school?

A: They are a little batty!

Q: Why did King Arthur stay up until 2:00 a.m.?

A: He was a knight owl.

Q: What do monkeys like to drink?

A: Ape-ple juice!

Q: What happened when the corn flew on the airplane?

A: Its ears popped.

Q: Why can't you ever get a wig for free?

A: Because you always have toupee!

Q: Why did the skunk have to get a new piggy bank?

A: It had a lot of scents!

Q: Why did the astronaut break up with his girlfriend?

A: He needed some space!

Q: Why did the librarian take some time off work?

A: She was overdue for a vacation!

Would you rather

eat ten hot dogs

or

chow down on ten hamburgers?

Would you rather

have a stuffy nose

or

have your ears plugged?

Would you rather

spend a thousand dollars in one place

or

have five hundred dollars to spend all

over town?

Would you rather

have a parent who is famous

or

have a famous brother or sister?

Would you rather

build a LEGO house big enough to live

in

or

build a LEGO spaceship big enough to

fly in?

Would you rather

go to the Super Bowl

or

go to the Academy Awards?

Would you rather

have six fingers on each hand

or

six toes on both your feet?

Would you rather

eat pizza with a scoop of ice cream

or

have ice cream with cheese on top?

Would you rather

have a nose that honks like a goose

or

have a laugh that barks like a dog?

Q: Where did the CEO practice woodworking?

A: In the boardroom!

Q: What kind of animal makes a great plumber?

A: A seal.

Q: What do you call a chimpanzee's brother?

A: A monkey's uncle!

Q: Why did the vampire keep falling out of the tree?

A: He couldn't get the hang of it!

Q: Why do soccer players throw the best parties?

A: They know how to get the ball rolling.

Q: What did the ladybug say to the firefly?

A: "Way to glow!"

Q: How did Spider-Man learn how to climb buildings?

A: From a website!

Knock, knock.

Who's there?

Slime.

Slime who?

Slime for another joke!

Q: Why did the orchestra go to the auto shop?

A: They needed a tune-up!

Knock, knock.

Who's there?

Italy.

Italy who?

Italy a while before I can come back.

Q: Why did the boy start a lawn-mowing business?

A: He heard it was cutting edge!

Q: Why are sea monsters so smart?

A: They're always thinking deep thoughts!

Q: What did the man say when he met an alien?

A: "Far out!"

Q: How did the astronaut feel when she landed on Mars?

A: Over the moon!

Q: Why did the firefly lie down for a nap?

A: It was feeling light-headed!

Q: What did the lettuce say to the tomato in the race?

A: "You'd better ketchup!"

Would you rather

swim with the mermaids

or

ride a unicorn?

Would you rather

take a bath in a tub of pancake batter

or

take a syrup shower?

111

Would you rather

walk backward all the time

or

always sit upside down?

Q: Why did the groundhogs get married?

A: They dug each other!

Q: What kind of bug comes out in a storm?

A: A lightning bug!

Q: Why did the plumber go on vacation?

A: Because he was drained!

Q: Why did the firefighter buy a horse?

A: She wanted to blaze a new trail!

Q: Why did the boy go fly-fishing every day?

A: Once he tried it, he was hooked!

Q: Why did the boy save his watermelon seed?

A: They were one in a melon!

Q: Why should everybody adopt a pet?

A: They help you stay paws-itive!

Q: What did the crocodile say to the slow swimmer?

A: "Make it snappy!"

Q: Why don't fish give in to peer pressure?

A: They know how to swim against the stream!

Q: Why did the farmer get up early to milk the cows?

A: He was moo-tivated!

Q: Why did the squirrel get sent to the principal's office?

A: It was driving its teacher nuts!

Q: What do you call it when someone copies your moves in checkers?

A: Play-giarism!

Q: What does Mario say when he goes on a roller coaster?

A: "Wii!"

Q: What happened when the eagle stole a watch?

A: Time flew by!

Q: What do you get when you cross a dinosaur and a dictionary?

A: A thesaurus!

Q: What word becomes shorter after you add two letters to it?

A: Short.

Q: Why did Dracula's girlfriend break up with him?

A: She thought he was a pain in the neck!

Q: Why does everybody love Spider-Man?

A: Because he's Marvel-ous!

Q: What do you get when you hide your fruit underground?

A: Straw-buries!

Q: Why couldn't the chef decide what to make for dinner?

A: He kept stewing over it!

Q: What do you call rich rabbits?

A: Million-hares!

Q: Why was the butcher successful?

A: He was a cut above the rest!

Would you rather

take a math quiz every day of the week

or

take a spelling test every day?

Would you rather

spend all day at the beach

or

spend the day at the pool?

Q: What is always in front of you but can never be seen?

A: Your future.

Q: Dan's parents have three kids: Snap, Crackle, and what's the name of the third child?

A: Dan!

Q: What happened when the cowboy saw a poisonous snake?

A: He was rattled!

Would you rather

stay awake for twenty-four hours

or

stay in bed for twenty-four hours?

Would you rather

run a marathon

or

swim across a lake?

Q: What do you call a horse who says "moo"?

A: A cow-nterfeit.

Q: What do you call a cow who can fly?

A: Legen-dairy!

Q: Why was the crab limping?

A: It pulled a mussel.

Knock, knock.

Who's there?

Owl.

Owl who?

Owl you need is love!

Q: Why did the dentist sign up for a marathon?

A: She wanted to run for twenty-six smiles!

Q: What do geometry teachers like to eat?

A: Three square meals per day.

Q: What do you get when a pig has a cold?

A: Ham-boogers.

Q: Why didn't the lobster want to hide in the cave?

A: It was claw-strophobic.

Q: What do boxers eat for breakfast?

A: Black-and-blueberries!

Q: How did the baker fix her broken bowl?

A: She used paste-ries!

Q: What do you call a very large flea?

A: Gigan-tick!

Q: Why did the carpenter put the wood in the corner?

A: It was knotty!

Q: Why didn't the archer have any friends?

A: He was too arrow-gant!

Q: Why did the cat smell so nice?

A: It used purr-fume!

Q: Why did the duck go to the ballet?

A: To see the Nut-quacker!

Q: Where did the school cafeteria get its vegetables?

A: From the kinder-garden.

Q: Why did the librarian go fishing?

A: She had a lot of bookworms!

Q: Why couldn't the electrician change a light bulb?

A: He wasn't very bright!

Q: What is the noisiest vegetable?

A: A bell pepper.

Would you rather

have a fin like a shark

or

a horn like a rhino?

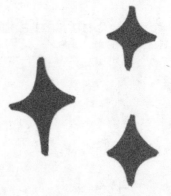

Would you rather

get fifty mosquito bites

or

five bee stings?

Q: What happens if you burn a gorilla's breakfast?

A: You're toast!

Q: What monsters are good at math?

A: None, unless you Count Dracula.

Q: **What happened when the fruits had a baby?**

A: They became pear-ents.

Knock, knock.

Who's there?

Handsome.

Handsome who?

Handsome of your jokes my way!

Would you rather

be the principal at your school

or

be the gym teacher?

Would you rather

have 360-degree vision like a fly

or

jump twenty times your height like a

grasshopper?

Would you rather

explore a cave underground

or

explore a shipwreck under the sea?

Would you rather

run out of toilet paper

or

run out of toothpaste?

134

Would you rather

play a game of hide-and-seek

or

play a game of tag?

Q: Why did the thermometer go back to college?

A: It wanted more degrees!

Q: What do ghosts wear in a storm?

A: Their rain boo-ts!

Q: Why did the man steal the farmer's cows?

A: He wanted to milk him for all he was worth!

Q: Why did the pig farmer call the fire department?

A: To save his bacon!

Q: Why do pigs make great comedians?

A: They like to ham it up!

Q: Why did the monkey run away from the zoo?

A: It was going bananas!

Q: What did the fisherman say to the trout?

A: "Catch you later!"

Q: Why did the astronauts get married?

A: He promised he'd give her the moon!

Would you rather

walk across a tightrope

or

swing from a trapeze?

Would you rather

never have any homework

or

never have to clean your room?

Would you rather

redecorate your whole room

or

get all new clothes?

Would you rather

get hit with snowballs

or

get hit with water balloons?

Would you rather

play a game of catch

or

play a game of cards?

- -

Would you rather

learn how to juggle

or

learn how to perform magic tricks?

Would you rather

have big hands and little feet

or

have little hands and big feet?

Q: **What happened to the detective in a hurricane?**

A: His cover was blown!

Q: **Why did the reporter get an ice-cream cone?**

A: He wanted to get the scoop!

Q: **How does it feel to throw a pumpkin off the roof?**

A: Smashing!

- -

Would you rather

mop the floor every day

or

wash all the dishes each day?

Q: What happens if you knock the pickles onto the floor?

A: It's a jarring experience!

Q: Why do dogs make bad dancers?

A: They have two left feet.

Q: Why did the doctor tell the lamp to gain some weight?

A: Because it was too light!

Q: What do rabbits wear in the kitchen?

A: Hare nets.

Q: How do you get an astronaut's baby to stop crying?

A: You comet down!

Knock, knock.

Who's there?

Alex.

Alex who?

Alex-plain it later!

Q: Why couldn't the boy have soda anymore?

A: He failed his pop quiz.

Q: When is a good time to have a peanut butter sandwich?

A: In a traffic jam.

Q: Why did the lady stop going to the butcher?

A: He gave her the cold shoulder!

Q: What's easy to catch in the winter but hard to throw?

A: A cold.

Q: How do you see a volcano in the dark?

A: With a lava lamp.

Q: Why do snakes make great comedians?

A: Because they're hiss-terical.

Q: What's a cowgirl's favorite plant?

A: A rodeo-dendron.

Would you rather

be an acrobat in the circus

or

be a clown in the circus?

Q: Why couldn't the race-car driver decide which way to go?

A: She was Indy-cisive.

Q: Why did the deer get braces?

A: It had buck teeth.

Q: What happened when the triceratops got strep throat?

A: It was dino-sore!

Would you rather

fall into a dunk tank

or

get a pie in the face?

Q: Why did the school choir go sailing?

A: They wanted to hit the high C's.

Q: What is a drummer's favorite vegetable?

A: Beets!

Q: How do you get a chicken to laugh?

A: Give it an egg yolk!

Q: How do you get a boulder to sleep?

A: You rock it!

Q: Why do boxers get good grades?

A: Because they're always hitting the books!

Q: Why did Dracula run away from the restaurant?

A: He accidentally ordered the stake!

Q: What kind of dog is always sad?

A: A melan-collie.

Q: What happened when the kangaroo stubbed its toe?

A: It was very unhoppy!

Q: What is a wasp's favorite sport?

A: Fris-bee!

Q: What's a farmer's favorite fairy tale?

A: Beauty and the Beets.

Q: Why couldn't the pirate play cards?

A: She was standing on the deck.

Q: What does a car wear to stay warm?

A: A hoodie!

Q: Why did the pepper put on a coat?

A: It was a little chili.

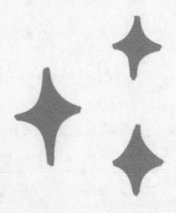

Q: Why did the horse fall over in the barn?

A: It wasn't stable!

Q: Why wouldn't the farmer go into the cornfield?

A: He was afraid of being stalked.

- -

Q: What happened when the farmer lost her pig?

A: She tractor down.

Q: What is a skunk's favorite kind of book?

A: A scratch-and-sniff!

Q: How did the bull feel about going in the barn?

A: He was beefing about it.

Knock, knock.

Who's there?

Tomatoes.

Tomatoes who?

I'm cold from my head to-ma-toes!

Q: Why was the boy so rowdy after dinner?

A: Because he was full of beans!

Q: How do you make a lemonade stand?

A: You take away its chair!

Q: Is it better to have uncles or aunts?

A: It's all relative!

Q: **What did one nose say to the other?**

A: "Long time no sneeze!"

Knock, knock.

Who's there?

Audi.

Audi who?

You Audi let me in so I can tell you a joke!

Q: How does a witch stay in shape?

A: With hex-ercize.

Q: What did the zombie say to her son?

A: "Chews your friends wisely!"

Q: Why was the train late to the station?

A: It lost track of time!

Q: What instrument did the skeleton play in the band?

A: The trom-bone!

Would you rather

eat a steak with a spoon

or

eat soup with a fork?

Would you rather

tie your shoes with licorice

or

button your shirt with jelly beans?

Q: What do daylight saving time and grasshoppers have in common?

A: They both spring forward.

Would you rather

eat three dog biscuits

or

give the dog your lunch?

Would you rather

visit the Eiffel Tower

or

see the Leaning Tower of Pisa?

Would you rather

spot the Loch Ness Monster

or

catch sight of Bigfoot?

Would you rather

open a gift bag

or

unwrap a present?

Q: Why can't you invite a crocodile to dinner?

A: Because it always chews with its mouth open.

Q: Why did the cowboy get a new horse?

A: It was a spur-of-the-moment decision.

Would you rather

learn to walk on stilts

or

ride a unicycle?

Would you rather

build a snow fort

or

build a sandcastle?

Would you rather

pet a snake

or

pet a tarantula?

Q: What kind of money is easy to burn?

A: In-cents.

Q: What happened when the girl swallowed her apple juice?

A: It went in-cider.

Q: What do dogs do when they're scared?

A: They flea!

Q: What do you call a dog wearing headphones?

A: It doesn't matter—he can't hear you anyway!

Q: What do you get when you cross a dog and a lobster?

A: A Doberman pincher.

Would you rather

give up your sense of taste

or

lose your sense of smell?

Would you rather

have a red nose like Rudolph

or

pointy ears like an elf?

Q: What do you call a dentist who cleans a crocodile's teeth?

A: CRAZY!

Q: What kind of flowers like to sing?

A: Pe-tune-ias.

Q: What do you eat when you're in the Navy?

A: Submarine sandwiches.

Would you rather

tour the Egyptian pyramids

or

explore the Amazon rainforest?

Would you rather

eat your hot foods cold

or

eat your cold foods hot?

Q: What can you serve but never eat?

A: A tennis ball.

Would you rather

bake cookies without a recipe

or

put together a LEGO kit without directions?

Would you rather

have Christmas with no cookies

or

have Thanksgiving without any pie?

Q: Why did the bird go to jail?

A: It was a robin!

Q: What do you call a bird with a high IQ?

A: Owl-bert Einstein.

Would you rather

have tree trunks for legs

or

have grass for your hair?

Would you rather

have a nose like Pinocchio

or

have ears like Dumbo?

Would you rather

glow in the dark

or

walk through walls?

Q: What happened when the meteorologist broke her arm?

A: She put it in a fore-cast.

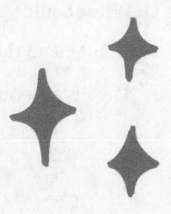

Q: What did the rancher ask the farmer?

A: "Have you herd the news?"

Q: Where does the composer store his sheet music?

A: In his Bach-pack.

Q: Why should you take your problems to the gym?

A: So you can work them out!

Would you rather

have your ears turn green when you're

jealous

or

have your nose turn purple when

you're surprised?

Q: Did you hear about the fight at

the gym?

A: They worked it out!

Q: Why wouldn't the vet remove the porcupine quills?

A: Because it would be pointless!

Knock, knock.

Who's there?

Hawaii.

Hawaii who?

I'm fine, Hawaii you?

Knock, knock.

Who's there?

Harrison.

Harrison who?

Harrison my head!

Q: Why do bumblebees fall in love?

A: Because beauty is in the eye of the

bee-holder!

Q: Why doesn't anybody like to wash the windows?

A: Because it's a pane!

Q: How do you get a dog to come to you?

A: You collar!

Q: What do you do if you can't afford to buy a boat?

A: Get somebody to float you the money!

Would you rather

eat out five days per week

or

enjoy five home-cooked meals every week?

Q: Why did the fisherman stop catching so many fish?

A: He wanted to scale back!

Q: What did the sow say to her piglets in the morning?

A: "Rise and swine!"

Q: Why don't crowbars mind their own business?

A: They're always prying!

Q: Why did the astronaut eat hamburgers on the moon?

A: Because they were meat-eor!

Q: Why did the snickerdoodle get straight A's?

A: It was one smart cookie!

Q: Why did the orchestra go to the gym?

A: So they could be as fit as a fiddle!

Q: Why don't bald guys ever have any fun?

A: Because they can't let their hair down!

Would you rather

have antennae like a cricket

or

have wings like a dragonfly?

Would you rather

cheer someone up with a present

or

give them a hug?

Would you rather

ride a bull in a rodeo

or

be the bull in a rodeo?

Would you rather

go bowling with a watermelon

or

play mini golf with apples?

Q: How do squirrels watch their movies?

A: On Nut-flix!

Q: Why did Frankenstein leave the party early?

A: He was bored stiff!

Would you rather

prank your friend with a whoopie

cushion

or

put a fake bug in their drink?

Would you rather

play Monopoly

or

play a game of Clue?

Would you rather

get a $5 allowance once a week

or

get $260 once a year?

Would you rather

wear swim fins on your feet all day

or

wear swim goggles all day?

Would you rather

go to the pool without swimming

or

go to the playground without playing?

Would you rather

go to a candy store

or

go to an ice-cream parlor?

Q: Why did the mummy go on vacation?

A: Because he was so wound up!

Q: Why don't people bring pickles to a party?

A: So there's never a dill moment!

Would you rather

get up at five in the morning

or

have to take an afternoon nap?

Would you rather

army-crawl everywhere

or

crab-walk wherever you go?

Would you rather

live in a doghouse

or

live in a birdcage?

Q: What did the leftovers say to the refrigerator?

A: "Drat, foiled again."

Q: Why did the rats follow the Pied Piper, but the mice didn't?

A: They thought his music was cheesy.

Q: When is a windshield like an ice-cream cake?

A: When it's defrosted!

Q: Why did Grandma quit ironing all the shirts?

A: She was running out of steam.

Q: Why did the trumpeters get in trouble in the band?

A: They had bad atti-toots!

Q: Why was the weaver so stressed out?

A: Her deadline was loom-ing!

Would you rather

take a summer vacation

or

take a winter vacation?

Would you rather

tell a funny joke

or

have a funny joke told to you?